Grandma, Lemay,

Love always

Chessie, Bitley, Luke &

James

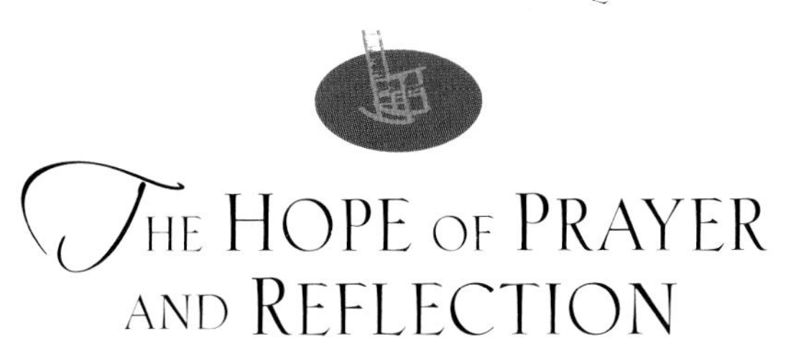

The Hope of Prayer and Reflection

INSPIRATION *from the* FRONT PORCH

by Roy Lessin & Heather Solum

ISBN 1-59310-654-8

Cover design by Greg Jackson, Jackson Design Co, llc

Cover and interior art by Barbara Pascolini

Published by Barbour Publishing, Inc., P.O. Box 719, Uhrichsville, Ohio 44683, www.barbourbooks.com

Our mission is to publish and distribute inspirational products offering exceptional value and biblical encouragement to the masses.

Printed in China.
5 4 3 2 1

The *Come Sit Awhile* gift book series is a collection of heartwarming stories, scriptures, recipes, quotes, prayers, and inspirational thoughts of hope and encouragement. We have chosen the theme of the front porch because it not only speaks of a place where people gather, relax, and enjoy the pleasures of each other's company, but it is also symbolic of a special place in our hearts where rest is found, where we enjoy the sweetness of God's presence, and where priceless memories are gathered and cherished always.

"In this manner, therefore, pray:

Our Father in heaven, hallowed be Your name.

Your kingdom come.

Your will be done on earth as it is in heaven.

Give us this day our daily bread.

And forgive us our debts, as we forgive our debtors.

And do not lead us into temptation,

But deliver us from the evil one.

For Yours is the kingdom and the power

and the glory forever. Amen."

MATTHEW 6:9–13 NKJV

When you sit on a front porch in spring-time, the heart becomes filled with expectation and pleasure as you gather in the wondrous nature around you—the crisp air, robins gathering twigs as they build their nests, the intoxicating smell of lilac bushes, tulips pushing toward the sky, raindrops bouncing off the rooftop, the budding of a dogwood tree, the brilliance of a redbud, and a thousand other joys that speak of the beginning of new things. It is from this rich treasury of creation that our hearts are moved to prayers of thankfulness, worship, and praise for all the blessings we've received from the One who has given us, abundantly, every good thing.

GOD. . .

GIVES US RICHLY

ALL THINGS TO ENJOY.

1 TIMOTHY 6:17 NKJV

When we receive blessings
from God as a result of answered prayer,
they come to us without regret or sorrow.
We can receive them with a peaceful heart
and enjoy them because
they come from the hand of
our loving Father.

A porch allows us to see things from a new perspective—take trees, for example. We fly over, drive past, and walk by trees all the time. As we pass, we casually observe their height and shape and sometimes admire their leaves or fruit. When we look at a tree while sitting on a front porch, other things come into view—the movement of the leaves in the wind, the subtle hues of color created by the sunlight, a delicately crafted nest tucked away in a protected corner, the activity of squirrels jumping from branch to branch, and the symphony of sounds that come from the birds that land on its branches.

When we reflect upon the scriptures, God's love allows us to see life from a new perspective. With His love in our hearts, a cloudy day can suddenly be filled with sunshine; a difficult situation can be covered in mercy; a trial can be bathed with grace; a setback can be turned for good; and a valley can be filled with new hope.

The time of business does not with me
differ from the time of prayer.
And in the noise and clutter of my kitchen,
while several persons are at the same time
calling for different things,
I possess God in as great tranquility
as if I were on my knees.

BROTHER LAWRENCE

"Stand still,

and consider the wondrous works of God."

JOB 37:14 NKJV

One of the special places to "stand still" and "consider" is the sanctuary of a front porch.

BE STILL,

AND KNOW THAT

I AM GOD.

PSALM 46:10 NKJV

Calmness—

God's serene and perpetual presence.

FREDERICK WILLIAM ROBERTSON

What sweet delights a quiet life affords.

HENRY DRUMMOND

Sit on your front porch
and reflect upon creation. . . .
It will tell you a lot about
the nature of its Creator.

Thus says God the LORD, who created the heavens and stretched them out, who spread forth the earth and that which comes from it,

Who gives breath to the people on it, and spirit to those who walk on it: "I, the LORD, have called You in righteousness,

And will hold Your hand; I will keep You and give You as a covenant to the people, as a light to the Gentiles."

ISAIAH 42:5–6 NKJV

A FRONT PORCH CAN BE
A STOPPING PLACE,
A QUIET PLACE,
A RESTING PLACE,
A REFLECTIVE PLACE,
AND A PRAYING PLACE.

The reflections on a day well spent
furnish us with joys more pleasing than
ten thousand triumphs.

THOMAS À KEMPIS

The Welcome Room

Ah, the front porches that have graced my life with memories! From my grandmother's small, whitewashed entrance in the hills of Kentucky to the well-kept, wrought iron porch I remember as a teen, porches defined family time in my growing-up years. The front porch was a place to eat messy watermelon after supper (without worries). . .a place to squeeze together on the swing with my mom and my sisters, laughing and talking about life. . .a place to relax and do nothing. . .a place to greet friends and visit with neighbors. . .

I have a lasting appreciation for the time my family spent in the "welcome room" of our home. There was comfort in the heart-to-heart conversations. There was joy in being away from the television and listening to each other intently. There was peace in being out-of-doors, yet contentedly still at home. . . .

I pray that I'll have the same wisdom God gave my parents and grandparents in knowing the value of simplicity—and the treasure of quiet time with family and friends. The sweetest keepsake of all is the praise embedded in every memory, because Jesus was the front-porch guest who brought the peace, the joy, and the love that we shared.

BONNIE RICKNER JENSEN

I sit on my front porch watching the sunrise of a new day. It is the middle of July, and the air is already warm. I think about the people I will soon need to see, the responsibilities I will face, and the decisions I will have to make. In the stillness of the moment, my heart lifts up a prayer. I sit quietly, knowing I am not alone. Gently, I hear the voice of my heavenly Father assuring me, "I am with you, and that is enough!"

"AS LONG AS THE EARTH ENDURES,
SEEDTIME AND HARVEST,
COLD AND HEAT,
SUMMER AND WINTER,
DAY AND NIGHT
WILL NEVER CEASE."

GENESIS 8:22 NIV

The things that we experience in life can often remind us of the changing seasons of the year.

In our springtime, our hearts gather new joys; in our summer, we go through growth and fruitfulness; in our fall, we gather the memories that we will cherish always; in our winter, we seek times of quiet reflection and prayer.

I REMEMBER THE DAYS
OF LONG AGO;
I MEDITATE ON ALL YOUR WORKS
AND CONSIDER WHAT
YOUR HANDS HAVE DONE.

PSALM 143:5 NIV

I love to sit out on my front porch during cool spring mornings and brisk autumn afternoons. Often, my porch becomes a front-row seat to God's outdoor cathedral. There is something wonderful about reading my Bible, praying, or reflecting on God's goodness when the sunlight floods the landscape, the trees bow in the wind, and all around me, birds sing their beautiful praises to God.

Praise the LORD. Praise God in his sanctuary;
praise him in his mighty heavens.
Praise him for his acts of power;
praise him for his surpassing greatness. . . .
Let everything that has breath praise the LORD.
Praise the LORD.

PSALM 150:1–2, 6 NIV

All creatures of our God and King,

Lift up your voice and sing,

Thou burning sun with golden beam,

Thou silver moon with softer gleam!

Thou rushing wind that art so strong,

Ye clouds that sail in heav'n along,

Thou rising morn, in praise rejoice,

Ye lights of evening find a voice!

ST. FRANCIS OF ASSISI

What a joy it is to learn to observe the quiet workings of the Holy Spirit in our hearts. Too often we expect God to speak to us through things that are big, packed with emotion, dramatic, or sensational. There are times when He does come like a mighty rushing wind, but more often, we find Him speaking to us in a still, small voice.

There is a signature of wisdom and power
impressed on the works of God,
which evidently distinguishes them from
the feeble imitations of men.
Not only the splendor of the sun,
but the glimmering light of the glowworm
proclaims His glory.

JOHN NEWTON

The Hiding Place

As a little girl, my favorite part of the porch was underneath it. It was a secret world where I loved to play and pretend. Our porch was high, standing about four feet above the ground, which left plenty of room for me to roam and hide. . . .

In my "under-the-porch world," I would dig

holes, build pretend houses out of sticks, dirt, and grass. . . I would imagine myself as the queen of my little domain. I was never afraid in my hiding place because of the company of my dog. He would always be with me, watching me play and standing guard ready to be my protector against unwanted intruders, especially snakes.

The only time my hiding place wasn't fun was when I entered and discovered that the chickens had gotten out and made their way under the porch. It was at that time that I really did wish I had that wonderful hiding place all to myself. . . .

JOAN HERBIG

SEE HOW HE HATH
EVERYWHERE MADE
THIS EARTH SO RICH AND FAIR;
HILL AND VALE
AND FRUITFUL LAND,
ALL THINGS LIVING,
SHOW HIS HAND.

JOACHIM NEANDER

You are my hiding place;
You shall preserve me from trouble;
You shall surround me with songs of deliverance.

PSALM 32:7 NKJV

God is our refuge and strength,
an ever-present help in trouble.

PSALM 46:1 NIV

He who dwells in the shelter
of the Most High will
rest in the shadow of the Almighty.

PSALM 91:1 NIV

You are my refuge and my shield;
I have put my hope in your word.

PSALM 119:114 NIV

The Place of Prayer

Ever since I can remember, I wanted to be a mother. I cannot describe the disappointment and sense of despair I felt when I discovered that I could not have children. (Part of that pain was due to the value I placed on a family, having come from a large family of eight children.)

My husband and I lived in a tiny farmhouse during our early years of marriage. We would often sit outside on our front porch and discuss the options that faced us for growing our family. We talked about adoption and the possibility of trying some new drugs that were on the market. Nothing seemed quite right to us, and we couldn't settle on anything that totally satisfied us. . . .

One evening, I went out on the porch alone. Distraught, I sat on the porch rocker and cried and prayed. My prayer was like that of Hannah's as I unburdened my heart before the Lord. As time passed, I found myself placing everything in God's hands. I got up and entered the house in complete peace. I knew that whatever God wanted would be okay.

Eighteen months passed without a change. Then one morning I woke up sick to my stomach. The day passed, but the sickness was back again the following morning. With some concern, I went to the doctor to be examined. I stood bewildered at his statement. "Mrs. Beck, I believe you're pregnant!"

"How can that be?" I replied in wonder.

"Do you believe in miracles?" was his candid reply.

RAQUEL BECK

"I am the LORD,

the God of all mankind.

Is anything too hard for me?"

JEREMIAH 32:27 NIV

"Call to me and I will answer you

and tell you great and unsearchable things

you do not know."

JEREMIAH 33:3 NIV

NOT A WHISPER
OF TRUE PRAYER
IS EVER LOST.

A. B. SIMPSON

Ask, and it shall be given you;
seek, and ye shall find;
knock, and it shall be opened unto you.

MATTHEW 7:7 KJV

I know not by what methods rare,

But this I know: God answers prayer.

I know not if the blessing sought

Will come in just the guise I thought.

I leave my prayer to Him alone

Whose will is wiser than my own.

ELIZA M. HICKOK

GOD CALLS US

TO PRAY. . . .

HE LISTENS

AS WE PRAY. . . .

HE ANSWERS

WHEN WE PRAY.

Intimacy

It was one of those moments you treasure for a lifetime. Unrehearsed. Spontaneous. Wonderful. There were four of us—all coworkers, all friends, all wives and mothers with burdens of our own. We were staying together at a women's conference, and our housing included a screened-in back porch. One evening after the meetings ended, we all found ourselves gathering on the porch. The fresh air was delightful. Each of us "cozied up" in a porch chair and quietly enjoyed the stillness. Within moments a gentle rain began to fall, and our hearts were slowly being drawn out to each other. One word led to the next, one feeling led to another, and we soon were emerged in intimate conversation. It was the highlight of the trip and deposited more into my heart than all the meetings we attended at the conference.

KAY EMERY

Jesus does more than give us salvation;

He is Salvation.

He does more than point the way;

He is the Way.

He does more than speak the truth;

He is the Truth.

He does more than give us life;

He is the Life.

At times God may seem slow in answering prayer, but He is never late.

But the angel said unto him,

Fear not, Zacharias:

for thy prayer is heard;

and thy wife Elisabeth shall bear thee a son,

and thou shalt call his name John.

LUKE 1:13 KJV

Any time is the right time to pray.

Rejoicing in hope;

patient in tribulation;

continuing instant in prayer. . .

ROMANS 12:12 KJV

TENDERLY

God keeps you close to His heart.

PRAYERFULLY

Your name is on His lips.

WATCHFULLY

He never lets you out of His sight.

The Father waits to hear every prayer of faith. He wants to give us whatever we ask for in Jesus' name. God intends prayer to have an answer, and no one has yet fully conceived what God will do for the child who believes that His prayer will be heard. God hears prayer.

ANDREW MURRAY

Prayer is the voice of faith speaking
and the hand of faith
receiving the good things
that are in the Father's heart to give.

Before you decide, pray about it.

A Parent's Prayer

Lord, as my children grow, help me train them with:

Vision—so they may discover all You made them to be.

Discipline—so their hearts may be tender and yielded to You.

Wisdom—so they will make good choices and hold right values.

Faith—so they will live free from fear and depend on You for all things.

Truth—so they will grow strong in character and in favor with You.

Love—so their hearts will come to know Your heart and express that love to others.

Everything by prayer!

God welcomes your prayers.

Let us therefore come boldly
to the throne of grace,
that we may obtain mercy
and find grace
to help in time of need.

HEBREWS 4:16 NKJV

Jesus went to the Father and sent the Holy Spirit to live in you.

His life will bring you great joy, for it is a life that is always pleasing to the Father.

"And He who sent Me
is with Me. . .
for I always do those things
that please Him."

JOHN 8:29 NKJV

"And I will pray the Father,

and He will give you another Helper,

that He may abide with you forever—

the Spirit of truth,

whom the world cannot receive,

because it neither sees Him nor knows Him;

but you know Him,

for He dwells with you and will be in you."

JOHN 14:16–17 NKJV

The greatest blessing that we have received from God is not His grace, His mercy, His forgiveness, nor His favor. This blessing is more wonderful than all the works and wonders that God performs on our behalf. It is the blessing of His presence.

How is this possible? It is the result of Jesus' prayer. The answer to His prayer was the coming of the Holy Spirit. The Holy Spirit's coming means that God is not only with you, but living in you. The God of all wisdom, power, goodness, and love not only reigns upon His throne, but He lives within your heart.

When you pray, you don't have to shout to get God's attention. He is not far away. He is closer to you than your own breath, and His life within you is more vital than your own heartbeat. He is in deep and personal communion with you. His Spirit is joined to your spirit. His Spirit is not close to you or next to you, but He is a part of you. His Spirit and your spirit are one. You can't get any closer than that!

BUT HE WHO IS
JOINED TO THE LORD
IS ONE SPIRIT WITH HIM.

1 CORINTHIANS 6:17 NKJV

Because of the intimacy that you have with God through the Holy Spirit, He is able to share His heart with you. His thoughts become your thoughts; His feelings become your feelings; and His desires become your desires. Prayer becomes an utterance of the deepest part of you touching the deepest part of Him.

"Your Father knows the things
you have need of before you ask Him."

MATTHEW 6:8 NKJV

Therefore I say unto you,
What things soever ye desire,
when ye pray, believe that ye receive them,
and ye shall have them.

MARK 11:24 KJV

God doesn't discover something new when we pray—He knows our needs even before we realize we have them. He is always ahead of us. God knows the prayers that we carry in our hearts long before they are ever spoken. This does not mean that we do not need to pray, but it means that we can pray in faith, believing that the answer is already on the way.

Nothing that is of interest to us is too small to interest Him. Many people do not believe this, but it is true. They think God is interested only in big things; but the same God that made the flaming suns and mighty worlds made the tiny insect, fashioned the lenses of its eyes, and painted with brightest colors its dainty wings. He is interested in the little quite as much as in the great. Therefore, we may bring everything to Him in prayer.

SAMUEL LOGAN BRENGLE

IN EVERYTHING
BY PRAYER AND SUPPLICATION,
WITH THANKSGIVING,
LET YOUR REQUESTS
BE MADE KNOWN TO GOD.

PHILIPPIANS 4:6 NKJV

Sometimes God delivers us from trials, and sometimes He allows us to walk through them. He does not do this to bring us defeat, but rather to allow us to learn things that are vital to our faith and trust in Him. There is always a beautiful rose that blooms at the end of every valley through which we walk. The name of the rose is "discovery," for its fragrance is the fresh revelation of how deeply Jesus loves us.

If someone could write
a cookbook on prayer,
every recipe would conclude
with these words:
"Mix with faith."

I REMEMBER

the days of old.

I PONDER

all your great works.

I THINK ABOUT

what you have done.

PSALM 143:5 NLT

A little boy was once asked, "Do you like being five more than you liked being four years old?"

The little boy thought for a moment and replied, "We can't go back; we can only go forward."

God doesn't want us to go back to our past or to live in the past, but He does want us to remember what He has done for us in the past. The older you grow, the greater your "scrapbook of blessings" will become.

When you lie awake, don't count sheep;

count your blessings.

I lie awake thinking of you,

meditating on you through the night.

PSALM 63:6 NLT

A Father's Prayer

Lord, grant me Your wisdom so that I may guide
my children with understanding;
teach me Your truth so that I may lay strong
foundations within them;
fill me with Your compassion so that my footsteps
will leave a path worth following;
keep me close to Your heart
so that all my responses
will be motivated by love.

A Mother's Prayer

Lord, in busy times keep me peaceful;
in needy times keep me content;
in difficult times keep me pleasant;
in disappointing times keep me hopeful;
in active times keep me balanced;
in teaching times keep me patient;
in all things keep me true.

IN THE MORNING,
PLACE YOUR ELBOWS
ON THE WINDOWSILL OF HEAVEN
AND GAZE UPON YOUR LORD,
AND IN THE BEAUTY OF
THAT VISION GO FORTH
TO MEET THE DAY.

UNKNOWN

PRAY PRIVATELY.

MATTHEW 14:23

Pray publicly.

ACTS 2:42

Pray constantly.

LUKE 18:1

Pray boldly.

HEBREWS 4:16

PRAY IN THE SPIRIT.

EPHESIANS 6:18

Pray in faith.

JAMES 1:6

Pray in confidence.

1 JOHN 5:14

Pray in earnest.

1 THESSALONIANS 3:10

Pray with praise.

PSALM 66:17

Pray with thankfulness.

COLOSSIANS 4:2

Pray with tears.

JEREMIAH 31:9

PRAY WITH JOY.

PHILIPPIANS 1:4

PRAY FOR PROVISIONS.

MATTHEW 6:11

Pray for victory.

MATTHEW 6:13

Pray for grace.

HEBREWS 4:16

Pray for wisdom.

JAMES 1:5

Whatsoever things are true,

whatsoever things are honest,

whatsoever things are just,

whatsoever things are pure,

whatsoever things are lovely,

whatsoever things are of good report;

if there be any virtue,

and if there be any praise,

think on these things.

PHILIPPIANS 4:8 KJV

Things that are true:

GOD'S NAMES. . .

Think about the meaning of each one.

GOD'S WORDS. . .

Think about their authority and power.

GOD'S WISDOM. . .

Think about how trustworthy He is.

GOD'S SPIRIT. . .

Think about His gentle and comforting ways.

GOD'S SON. . .

Think about what it means to have Him as your Savior.

Things that are honest:

GOD'S HONOR. . .

Think about His worthiness.

GOD'S PURPOSES. . .

Think about His eternal plan.

GOD'S PATHS. . .

Think about the benefits of following Him.

GOD'S COUNSEL. . .

Think about the things He has spoken to your heart.

GOD'S GUIDANCE. . .

Think about how He has directed your life.

Things that are just:

GOD'S JUDGMENTS. . .

Think about His majesty.

GOD'S DECISIONS. . .

Think about His will.

GOD'S DEALINGS. . .

Think about His ways with you.

GOD'S RESPONSES. . .

Think about His longsuffering and patience.

GOD'S ACTIONS. . .

Think about the times
He has shown
Himself
faithful.

Things that are pure:

GOD'S CHARACTER. . .

Think about His attributes.

GOD'S NATURE. . .

Think about His goodness and kindness.

GOD'S WORDS. . .

Think about His wisdom.

GOD'S MOTIVES. . .

Think about His desire to bless you.

GOD'S THOUGHTS. . .

Think about His endless thoughts toward you.

Things that are lovely:

GOD'S WAYS. . .

Think about all He has done.

GOD'S HOLINESS. . .

Think about His beauty.

GOD'S COUNTENANCE. . .

Think about His smile upon you.

GOD'S HEART. . .

Think about His boundless love.

GOD'S GLORY. . .

Think about His greatness.

Things that are of good report:

GOD'S CREATION. . .

Think about the beauty that surrounds you.

GOD'S REDEMPTION. . .

Think about what Jesus did for you.

GOD'S PROMISES. . .

Think about all that is yours because you are His.

GOD'S KINGDOM. . .

Think about His reign and rule.

GOD'S COVENANTS. . .

Think of all the blessings of His grace.

Sweet hour of prayer, sweet hour of prayer,
Thy wings shall my petition bear
To Him whose truth and faithfulness
Engage the waiting soul to bless.
And since He bids me seek His face,
Believe His word, and trust His grace,
I'll cast on Him my every care
And wait for thee, sweet hour of prayer!

WILLIAM W. WALFORD

IN PRAYER OUR WEAKNESS IS
LINKED TO ALMIGHTINESS,
OUR IGNORANCE TO
INFINITE WISDOM,
OUR NEED WITH
THE CHANNEL OF
UNSEEN RESOURCES.

HENRY GARIEPY

We pray with the unreserve of little children.
There is nothing about which we may not pray.
We pray as His children,
and we trust Him as our heavenly Father.
His answer will transcend our asking.

SAMUEL CHARWICK

I was sitting on my front porch on a warm, humid afternoon. The wind's intensity began to increase as it pushed its way through the trees that surrounded the front yard. The sky began to darken, and the sound of thunder rumbled nearby. Within minutes the first raindrops began to splash upon the rose petals. It was the beginning of a delightful summer rainstorm. As the storm passed, I was instantly refreshed by the changes the storm created. The sky was clear. The wind was calm. The humidity was broken. Delightful fragrances filled the air. Everything was fresh and renewed.

The rainstorm caused me to reflect upon

the needs in all of our lives. Each of us goes through the heat and humidity of trials and difficulties, but God is faithful to bring us the refreshing we need. His Spirit is the wind that cools us and the water that washes us. He delights in making us clean and fragrant with the renewing of His grace.

The inward man is renewed day by day.

2 CORINTHIANS 4:16 KJV

Great is his faithfulness;

his mercies begin afresh each day.

LAMENTATIONS 3:23 NLT

Unanswered yet!

Though when you first presented

This one petition at the Father's throne

It seemed you could not wait the time of asking

So urgent was the heart to make it known;

Though years have passed since then, do not despair

The Lord will answer you—sometime—somewhere.

E. B. BROWNING

IN PRAYER,

Jesus is your Intercessor;

IN TROUBLE,

He is your Comforter;

IN GUIDANCE,

He is your Counselor;

IN INSTRUCTION,

He is your Teacher;

IN LIFE,

He is your Lord;

IN RELATIONSHIP,

He is your Friend.

We can be sure of God's promises because of His character and His attributes. He never makes a promise He can't keep.

God keeps His promises because

He has the power to do what He has said.

God keeps His promises because

He doesn't change His mind about what He has said.

God keeps His promises because

He never forgets what He has said.

THERE'S NOT A PROMISE
GOD'S EVER BROKEN;
NOTHING'S FAILED THAT HE HAS SAID.
HE WILL NOT FORSAKE YOU;
LIKE THE SPARROW, YOU'LL BE FED.
GOD WILL NOT FAIL YOU;
HE WILL NOT LEAVE YOU ALONE.
GOD WILL NOT FAIL YOU;
HE DOES NOT FORSAKE HIS OWN.

REFLECT UPON YOUR BLESSINGS;
God has been good to you.
REFLECT UPON YOUR TRIALS;
His comfort has been there, too.
REFLECT UPON HIS MERCIES;
they're new to you each day.
REFLECT UPON HIS LOVELINESS;
it will never fade away.

When we look back and reflect upon our lives, we discover that our sweetest memories and richest treasures are found in the things that God has done for us. We recall our joys and remember how good He was. . .we recall our tears and remember how comforting He was. . . we recall our shortcomings and remember how merciful He was. . .we recall our fears and remember how loving He was. . .we recall our trials and remember how caring He was.

I RECALL
ALL YOU HAVE DONE,
O LORD;
I REMEMBER
YOUR WONDERFUL DEEDS.

PSALM 77:11 NLT